THE YOUNG LIFE
OF SAINT MARIA FAUSTINA

AUTHOR
Claire Jordan Mohan

ILLUSTRATOR
Jane Robbins

Marians of the Immaculate Conception
Stockbridge, Massachusetts 01263

2000

Library of Congress Catalog Card Number 99-75159
ISBN 0-944203-36-1

Editing and Proofreading by David Came, Stephen LaChance, and Mary Ellen McDonald

Typesetting and Design by Elizabeth Kulas

Cover Design by Elizabeth Kulas,
based on illustration of Saint Maria Faustina by Jane Robbins

Illustrations throughout text by Jane Robbins

Note to the reader: The full religious name of Saint Maria Faustina was Sister Maria Faustina of the Most Blessed Sacrament. Her religious name reflected her deep devotion to Jesus in the Most Holy Eucharist. (In the world, she was known by her baptismal name, Helena Kowalska.)

Printed in the United States of America by the Marian Press,
Stockbridge, Massachusetts 01263

Available from:
Marian Helpers Center
Stockbridge, MA 01263

Prayer Line: 1-800-804-3823
Order Line: 1-800-462-7426
Website: www.marian.org

CONTENTS

To my husband, Bob.

"GLADNESS OF THE HEART
IS THE LIFE OF A MAN, AND
THE JOYFULNESS OF A MAN
PROLONGETH HIS DAYS."

~Sirach 30:22

SAINT MARIA FAUSTINA

"I AM LOVE AND MERCY ITSELF. WHEN A SOUL APPROACHES ME WITH TRUST, I FILL IT WITH SUCH AN ABUNDANCE OF GRACES THAT IT CANNOT CONTAIN THEM WITHIN ITSELF, BUT RADIATES THEM TO OTHER SOULS."

Diary of Saint Maria Faustina, 1074

THE "LIGHT"

"O my Lord, inflame my heart with love for You, that my spirit may not grow weary amidst the storms."

DIARY, 94

She knew she wasn't crazy. Yet, others would later say it was an act of insanity. Why would she startle everyone like that? No one else had been aware of anything out of the ordinary. She was playing with Joey, the little boy she babysat, catching a ball and dancing around the courtyard having fun. It was a normal day. The sky was clear. It was warm and sunny.

Helen was "in service" which meant that she had the position of a maid. She worked for Mr. and Mrs. Bryszewski, helping with their home and children. They were friends of her parents and owned a bakery in Aleksandrow, a town not far from her home. She could see her family whenever she wanted.

She was happy working there doing much the same as she had done at home — helping with the house and caring for young children. At home she was the third oldest child of eight children — six girls and two boys. Housework and child care were second nature to her.

Helen always seemed to think things through. Money and clothing were scarce in her family and the girls had to share their Sunday best. Since Helen wanted nice clothes so she could go to church every Sunday, she begged her parents to allow her to leave home and find work as her two older sisters had done.

She was a cheerful girl, pleasant to be around, not given to outbursts, although she was lively, joyous, and a little impulsive by nature. Her pale, freckled face was lightened by frequent smiles and everyone said she was a level-headed girl. She knew she was. Yet, on this day, she had seen a flashing light and in a rare outburst she had screamed, "Fire, fire!" and then passed out. She frightened all around her. When she awoke, she was frightened too! What did it mean? What was the "light"?

She had been sure there was a fire in the courtyard. Everyone ran to the scene. Everywhere there was confusion. The bread was being put into the bake-oven at that moment. The bakers dropped the loaves! That was the last thing she saw as she fell in a heap upon the ground.

"She will be all right. She's awakening now," she heard someone say as she was coming to. Through fluttering eyelashes, she saw the dark figure shake his head in confusion. "What is going on? What did I do?" she questioned herself. A doctor was never called unless it was really serious. Yet, here was one staring at her and feeling her pulse! Her employers must be greatly concerned.

"Is she insane?" Mr. Bryszewski asked worriedly. How could she reassure them? She sat up quickly and shook her head, the thick auburn-colored braid swinging toward them. "I'm sorry," she uttered, "I don't know what happened." Mrs. Bryszewski took her hand and offered her a sip of water. "Come inside, dear, and lie down; perhaps that will clear your mind. You'll feel better after a little rest."

Helen did as she was instructed and was led inside the home. As she lay in the darkened room, left alone to her thoughts, Helen recalled a strange experience she had had when she was seven years old. It was during the exposition of the Blessed Sacrament. As she gazed up at Jesus in the golden monstrance, a strange feeling had passed through her body. It was like a deep shiver that shook her from her head to her feet. It was not frightening as this moment today had been. It was more a time of joy in her heart — a feeling of deep love.

Somehow she knew this "light" today was from God, but didn't quite understand its meaning. She needed time to think it through. Was God calling her? What did He want her to do? Was this an angel? "Dear God," she prayed, "tell me what this is all about."

As she lay on the soft cot, hearing the murmuring of others in the courtyard through the open window, she continued to pray for understanding.

Very early in life Helen had been taught to say short prayers. As a little child she was drawn to seek the things of heaven, following the example of her deeply religious parents. There was that vivid dream she had had when she was only five years old. The next morning she had described it in detail to her mother.

"I was walking hand in hand with the Mother of God in a beautiful garden." And many times after that she would awake during the night and sit up in bed remembering the beauty of the flowers and the love she had felt for Mary. When her mother would walk into the room and see her praying, she would say, "Helen, go back to sleep or you'll lose your mind." "Oh no, mother," she would answer, "my guardian angel must be waking me to pray."

The girl was now fifteen years old. Old enough to understand. She got up from the bed and knelt at its side. She opened up the curtains and looked skyward. Suddenly, she knew what she must do. It was as if a voice spoke to her.

Hours later, Mrs. Bryszewski came to the room. "Helen," she announced, "you have a visitor." She went outside and was met by her sister Josephine. The Bryszewskis had sent word to her parents.

"What on earth happened?" her sister asked. "Mother and Father are worried sick about you."

Helen replied, "Josie, I saw a strange light. Don't ask me to explain it. Trust me. Tell Mama not to worry. I am not crazy, but I can't talk about it. Just tell them I will not be staying here long. When I come home, they'll understand."

She hugged her sister and they talked no more about it. After being convinced Helen was all right, Josephine walked home, still wondering about "the strange light."

A GIFT FROM HEAVEN

"Happy the soul that knows how to love unreservedly,
for in this lies its greatness."

DIARY, 997

SIXTEEN YEARS EARLIER ...
The sun had just gone down and a soft breeze fluttered the tops of the golden wheat waiting to be harvested. A pine tree whispered goodnight. It was the last week of August in Poland — a hot and muggy evening. Josephine and Genevieve were tired and puzzled. There was an air of expectancy throughout their house which they did not understand.

"I'm sleepy," Genevieve whined to her older sister, her tousled head leaning forward and her eyes almost closing.

"I'm tired, too," replied Josie.

The two small girls sat like little mice outside on the stone doorstep, long bored with chasing fireflies. It was past their bedtime. They always said night prayers and were settled in their cots by dusk. Now, it was dark. The evening star already brightened the sky, and no one was paying attention to them.

They were startled by footsteps on the walk. Their kind neighbor patted their heads as she strode past. They watched like sleepy cats as she lit a lantern, rang the cow bell forcefully, and hurried into the house.

The little girls left their perches like startled birds as their father hastened into the house with a worried look on his face. Suddenly, they heard a scream from inside the house and then, another strange cry.

Before they could enter, the door burst open. Out came their neighbor, her arms extended and a huge smile on her face. She was holding a soft pink blanket from which a little red face peeked.

"Oh, Papa, it's a baby!" they shouted, their eyes wide open as they gazed at the wonder before them.

"You have a new little daughter!" she exclaimed. Stanislaus looked relieved and rushed toward her. They heard him pray, "Dear God, I thank You for this child." He sighed and added softly so that they could barely hear, "Dear Lord, another girl! I thought You would send me a son."

Stanislaus and Marianna were married in 1892. They were poor country people who had a strong love for God. Stanislaus awoke before dawn each day to sing hymns and psalms of praise before he did his work.

They lived in a small, two-room stone and brick cottage along the roadside outside of town. They had ten acres of farm land and almost four acres of pasture for their three cows. Stan was a serious 25-year-old man when they married. He farmed in the evening and early morning before going to his job as a carpenter in the nearby village.

Marianna was a sweet, sensitive, hardworking young girl just eighteen years old who loved taking care of their home. She helped her husband all she could around the farm. At lunchtime, she would walk into town bringing him a hot lunch and then would go into the forest to collect firewood.

Young as they were, they longed for children. Each day they prayed, but their prayers were not answered until ten years after they were married. Then, to their great joy, a daughter, Josephine, was born. Just over a year later, another daughter arrived — and now, a third! — but a farmer needs sons, and looks forward to their help.

As Stanislaus and the two girls entered the room, Marianna smiled happily at them. Stan put his arms around her. The girls cautiously touched their baby sister who opened her tiny blue eyes to greet them.

"Oh, Stan, look at this little one," she cried. "Isn't she the prettiest baby you've ever seen? She came into this world so quickly, I barely knew she had arrived. Oh, Stan, she is special, I know. I am so thankful for her. See, the girls love her, too."

"You're right, Mari. True, I wished for a boy, but this little one is wonderful. Come, Josie and Genny, kneel beside Mama, and we will pray together."

And so Helen came into the world — a tiny, red-faced baby with blonde fuzz on her head who grew into a beautiful girl with strawberry-blonde hair, grey-green eyes, and a pale freckled complexion. She would be different from her brothers and sisters in appearance and in temperament from the very beginning.

FIRST HOLY COMMUNION

"The most solemn moment of my life is the moment when I receive Holy Communion. I long for each Holy Communion, and for every Holy Communion I give thanks to the Most Holy Trinity."

DIARY, 1804

The sky was still gray as she opened her eyes. The sounds of birds chirping called her from sleep. Helen crawled from under her covers and crept over her sisters to reach the window. The morning star winked at her. The rooster cock-a-doodled. She watched the rosy curtain of dawn slowly awaken the sky. The golden rays of sun appeared like the golden monstrance. Morning was finally here!

In the other room, Papa was singing. His deep voice swelled throughout the cottage. "Oh, how I love to hear the hymns and psalms," she thought. "It is music to my heart. Angels in heaven must sound like this." She sang the words softly along with her father.

"Hush, Stan," she heard her mother whisper. "You'll wake the children. They need their sleep."

"No, Marianna," he answered. "We both know they must feel God's love early each day."

And this day was special! Today Helen would make her first Holy Communion. She could barely stand still. She looked over in the corner at the beautiful white dress she would soon put on. Josie and Genny had worn it on their special day. Mama had created every stitch of it with her loving hands.

"Mama is wonderful," she thought. "She is such a good mother in every way! I am so lucky to have her." In the kitchen, Marianna was smiling almost as though she could read Helen's thoughts.

Each day of her life, as Helen had followed her mother around the house and farm, learning her duties, she also learned about Jesus. Marianna taught her her catechism and told her stories from the Bible. And Papa, too, made sure his children were good, obedient, and holy. At night they would sit by the fire as he read stories of the saints and missionaries.

Helen also went for instructions twice a week to prepare for Holy Communion. She studied hard. She was ready! "My heart is aching for Jesus," she said to herself.

All through her nine years, Helen had been surrounded with a deep spiritual feeling. Religion was the most important thing in the Kowalski family. Every moment was saturated by faith from the instant their father poured out his voice before dawn until bedtime when they would gather before the Madonna and whisper their goodnights.

Each season would bring special rituals which they learned to love. At Christmas there were the carols sung at dawn, and at night by the manger and the glowing tree. In Lent there were sacrifices followed by the joy of Easter Sunday Mass and baskets filled with flowers and decorated eggs.

In the springtime, Papa made a little May shrine attached to the pear tree standing outside their home. All the children decorated it with holy pictures and flowers and a statue of the Madonna. Each took a turn. On his or her day, the chosen child searched the orchard for the prettiest cherry or apple blossoms and greenest ivy to decorate the wreath that would crown Mary.

The Kowalskis and their neighbors would often gather at night to pray. There were only two wooden benches, so Helen, who always thought of others, would bring out stools so that all could be seated. The candles burned brightly and they lifted their hearts to their Creator in prayer and song.

Helen loved to pray and many times she would awaken during the night and sit up in bed. At times, it seemed a "light" had awakened her. She sometimes thought it was her guardian angel. She was puzzled, but she did not say much about it. She realized she was different from her sisters and brothers. She didn't confide in Josephine or any of the family. She told everything to God.

Helen's little heart was full of love. On Sunday evenings when they would attend Vespers, the small girl felt safe in the dark church. The candles glowed and the Golden Monstrance called her heart. The "light" seemed to surround her, but she couldn't understand. And she knew no one who could explain what she felt.

But this morning she knew what was happening. She felt the love of Jesus and her soul was waiting to receive Him.

"Oh Mama, I am so happy. Today I will finally have Jesus in my very own heart!" she cried.

The girls helped Helen to get ready. She put on the white dress. Her eyes sparkled and her brushed hair was like shining copper.

"Oh, Helen, you are so pretty! You look like an angel!" they declared.

When it was time to leave, she followed the old Polish custom of kissing her parents hands. All the children stood by the gate and waved to her, as if wishing her *bon voyage* as she set off down the dirt road on the short walk to the village. The trees sang as she passed, and she almost danced with joy to their music.

At the church, the boys and girls, lined up in procession according to their size, solemnly entered the chapel. They filed into the oak pews like soldiers following a drum beat. Some of the other girls, like distracted little birds, smoothed their skirts, and fussed with their hair. Helen folded her hands and waited.

She walked slowly up the aisle following one of her friends to the altar rail. As the priest placed the Host into her mouth, the organ played softly and Helen's heart sang with joy. She returned to her seat, placed her head in her hands, and felt alone with her God.

When Mass was over she started for home all alone, and deep in thought. The others walked in groups chatting happily. Her neighbor met her along the way and looked at her curiously.

"Helen, why aren't you going back with the other children?" she questioned. "Why are you alone?"

"Oh, Mrs. Krzyzanowski, I'm not alone. I'm going with Jesus," she replied politely. After a while, she caught up with her friend, Maria. Helen's eyes were shining, her voice a song.

"Maria, are you happy about today?" she asked.

"Yes, of course," said the friend. "Look at what a pretty dress I'm wearing."

Helen looked at her own beautiful dress and replied, "Oh, yes, and I'm happy to have received Jesus." Maria looked at her strangely and turned into her gate.

On nearing the cottage, Natalie ran to her. "Helen, how happy you look!" she exclaimed.

"Oh, Natalie, just wait until Jesus comes to you!" she answered.

The whole family was waiting. There was a surprise package from Mama and Papa. It was a little book — "A Child's Guide to Jesus" were the words printed in green on the shiny white cover. Her eyes filled with tears.

"Oh, Mama and Papa, thank you! It is just what I wanted!" she exclaimed, as she glanced through the pages happily. She

rushed over and kissed them.

Lunch was waiting and there was special food to honor the day. Mama had baked an apple cake. They all crowded around the table and Helen opened her new book and joyfully led them in prayers of thanksgiving.

Soon the sun was fading in the west, and it was bedtime. Helen took off her white dress, hung it carefully on the hanger, and put on her nightgown. Once again the window called her. She sat by the sill as she watched the rosy glow of sky turn pink and then gray. A sliver of moon hung in the dark. The evening star shone brightly. Helen, full of joy, said her prayers, crawled into bed, and went to sleep.

HELEN'S DILEMMA

"Great love can change small things into great ones, and it is only love which lends value to our actions."

DIARY, 303

Helen had a problem. It was a muggy Saturday evening in July. Josephine, Genevieve, Helen, Natalie, Stanislaus, Miecislaus, Mary, and their neighborhood friends had just finished a game of hide-and-seek in the wheat fields. Mrs. Gruskalski had called her children home. The Kowalskis were tired and bedraggled — their faces wet and sweaty from racing around.

The sun was low in the sky. After a cool drink from the well, they splashed their faces with the water, and collapsed in the shade by the side of the barn. The soft grass cushioned their tired bodies.

"Helen, tell us a story," begged Natalie.

Helen often amused her sisters and brothers this way. She was a gifted storyteller who embellished the tales of hermits and saints she had heard from their father. She would dramatize them and the children would hang onto her every word. She even suggested they all become hermits and live on roots and berries in the forest — and everyone readily agreed to join her! They leaned against the barn wall ready to be entertained, but could see that something was on her mind.

Finally, she said, "I want to go to church, too."

"What are you talking about, Lena?" asked Genevieve.

"Papa says the cows have to be put out to pasture before any of us can go to church tomorrow. I know there is only one Mass and we all can't go, what with taking the cows out to pasture, but there must be a way! I don't want to stay home with the animals when I can be in church with God."

"Well, Helen, you can't disobey Papa," Josephine said. "You would be in big trouble. You know how he thrashed Stanley just last week for breaking twigs from Mr. Gruskalski's willow tree."

"Yes, I am still sore," groaned Stanley patting the seat of his pants. Miecislaus shivered, glad that he had decided not to join his brother in that escapade.

"You know I would never do that," replied Helen. "I know Papa is very strict with us, but he just wants to teach us to be good. I am thinking of a way that will not upset him."

"Watch out when Helen thinks!" declared Natalie.

"Yes, Lena," said Josie, "I remember the time you started

feeling sorry about the poor people in the village. We'll never forget how you dressed in dirty rags and went around the village from house to house saying a prayer and asking for alms, just as if you were a penniless person yourself."

"And," added Stanley, "remember the time you decided to organize a raffle for the poor? You went around to all the neighbors asking them for small gifts, then wrote out lottery tickets, and sold them. You collected some money that you gave to Father Walter."

"And how about the time you had that little shop and made toys yourself and sold them for the poor," said Natalie. "You are always thinking of others and trying to be like Jesus. I know you love God, but this time you might be disappointed."

"Don't worry, Helen," said little Mary. "I know you can do anything! Mother says you have in-i-tia-tive," she said, straining to pronounce the word. "And she told me that means you figure out how to do things all by yourself!"

They all contemplated Helen's predicament. But before a plan could be devised, the sun had set, dark was falling, and there was a call from the cottage door.

"Come, children. It is time for night prayers," called their mother. Obediently, they rose to answer.

The house, shielded by the tall pine tree outside, was cool and comfortable. First, Papa led them in song. Their joyous voices, full of love, filled the room and resounded like an angelic choir.

Together, they knelt before the crucifix — Mama, Papa and all the children — while the littlest Kowalski, Wanda, slept in her mother's arms. After kisses goodnight, they climbed into bed and were soon fast asleep. Except Helen. She lay on her bed wracking her brain for a solution. She prayed for an answer. Finally it came to her!

She waited until her parents were asleep, then she quietly unlocked the bedroom window. In the morning before dawn, she awakened, tip-toed past her parents, and slipped out the opened window into the misty morning. Running to the barn, she silently undid the doors, unlocked the gates, and led the cows to pasture on the grassy path between the wheat.

When the sun rose, the family, awakened as usual by Papa's singing, came together for breakfast. Just as he was about to drink from his cup, Stanislaus looked out the window and noticed the open barn.

"Oh, My Lord! Marianna," he shouted, "someone has stolen our cows!"

They all ran outside. Suddenly, they heard someone singing.

"It's Helen!" Mama cried.

"I can't believe she would do this," her father bellowed. "Helen is bringing the cows home from the far end of the field. Now they will ruin my wheat crop. What can she be thinking? She must be punished for this!"

He unbuckled his leather belt and held it ready to punish his daughter. Instead, as he walked towards her, he saw the three cows tied to one rope, the grass on the pathway eaten, but not a blade of wheat touched on either side. He hid the belt behind his back.

"Papa," she called to him, "may I go to Mass today?"

"Oh, yes, Helen, you may," he answered. "But, daughter, you sure gave me a scare. Don't ever do that again!"

Smiling happily, she took the cows to the barn and began to milk them. She could go to Mass!

Once World War I began, all of Poland suffered destruction, great famine, and poverty. Their homeland had been a battlefield and the four years of conflict had left the country ravaged.

The Kowalski family was almost destitute and there was not enough Sunday-best clothing. The girls lent each other their dresses, working out the order in which each would wear the best. Helen knew her parents had money problems, so she did not ask for new clothes. As the third daughter, this meant she often was the one to remain at home while the others went to church. She knew Jesus would not want her to be selfish, so she did not complain.

Instead, she found her own way to be alone with Jesus. There was a tranquil spot in a corner of the garden near the orchard. Alone and filled with peace, she sat on a cracked wooden bench, holding her prayer book and whispering the Sunday prayers. Tall beech trees bent their branches to welcome her. Birds nesting in the shrubs joined her in praising God.

"Helen," her mother often called, but she pretended not to hear.

Afterward, she would explain as she kissed her mother's hands, "Mama, I am not being disobedient. It is just I know Jesus would be angry if I left Him."

Her loving mother understood and knew that whenever Helen did not go to church, it would be the same. She realized that this special child, as young as she was, had come to the deeper realization that loving and serving God was the most important thing in Life.

"Marianna, what do you think of Helen?" Stanislaus inquired one day.

"Stan, our Helen is different, and has been since the moment she was born," her mother answered. "There is something about her that makes me wonder. She always solves any problem in an unique way — but it always seems to be God's way. Stanley, we must pray to understand and treasure her, for she is a gift."

A YOUNG STUDENT

"My life at present flows on in peaceful awareness of God."

DIARY, 887

All the students had attempted to memorize the poem. Their teacher, Mr. Lazinki, listened intently as each recited it. Some stuttered, some stumbled. One voice stood out.

"Helen," he stated. "You must say the poem for the principal. He will decide. I think you will be the one!"

The other boys and girls clapped their hands. They all loved their fellow student and knew she was the best. Mr. Lazinki sent for the principal. In minutes he was there, ready to hear the recitation. He sat at the teacher's oak desk, his head leaning on his hand and his eyes slightly closed as he concentrated.

Helen repeated her beautiful recitation and when she had finished, he said, "Next week the inspector will be coming. You will recite 'The Father's Return' for him. We are very proud of you and the inspector will know we are doing a good job."

Helen was pleased. She was twelve years old and only in second grade — not through her own fault. World War I had totally disorganized the life of the people living in the war zone. Schools had been closed and only opened when things returned to normal.

Helen's father had taught her how to read, so she was a little more advanced than the other children her age. She was a good student who studied willingly, and she had a very good memory.

The inspector arrived early Monday morning. The classroom was ready. All week the students had prepared. Copies of their best work were displayed. The windows were sparkling and not a speck of dirt or chalk dust littered the floor. The children, too, were fresh and bright — their hair neatly combed and their clothes spotless.

The inspector was a stern-looking man with a silver beard and hair, carrying a cane. He strode into the room with the dignified principal at his side. The children quickly stood to greet him and, at their teacher's direction, proudly sang their national anthem. The principal stood at the front of the room. He spoke words of welcome and introduced each of the boys and girls. Then came the moment they were waiting for.

"Now who can recite Adam Mickiewicz's famous poem, 'The Father's Return'?" he asked.

Everyone looked at Helen. The principal called her name. Though her stomach was full of butterflies, she caught her breath, stood up tall, and confidently recited the many stanzas of the poem.

As she spoke the last word, the inspector turned to the principal, "Your students are very bright," he said. "I commend your teachers."

Looking at Helen and nodding his silver head, he said with a smile, "Fine job, young lady! Here, this is your reward. I hope you will like it."

Helen's eyes danced as she returned his smile. Shaking his hand, she accepted the praise and the book of Polish poets, then returned to her seat. Glancing at the title, she knew it would be fun reading this to her brothers and sisters.

"In the evening when all our chores are done, I can dramatize them and make the children laugh or cry," she thought.

Unfortunately, Helen's education was cut short. After she had studied only two terms, the principal came into the classroom and made a shocking announcement.

"The authorities have decided the older children have to leave the school so that there will be room for the younger children," he stated.

Some of the children cheered, some of them complained, but Helen had tears in her eyes.

"Well, I know what I must do," she told the trees as she walked home through the forest. "I must read all I can and then I will teach the little children what I have learned."

And every chance she got, this is what she did, though she was busy helping her mother.

With such a large family, there was plenty of wash to be done and hung out, food to be cooked, and so much to do for the little ones. And around the farm, the cows still needed to be milked and the chickens needed to be fed. The nests had to be checked every morning for eggs and the rooster had to be kept away from the hen house.

As she did all these things, she sang the hymns so familiar to her. Her mind and heart were with Jesus. At night she still awoke and prayed. One time she confided in her parents, "Mama, I still see the bright lights I told you about. I don't know what they are, but they make me feel close to God."

"Helen," was the reply, "Papa and I have discussed this. You must stop imagining these things. Stop talking such nonsense!"

She did stop talking about them, but couldn't stop thinking about them.

Helen was growing into her teens and she always tried to please her parents — and she succeeded. Although her sisters and brothers managed to get into mischief and get punished, Helen was always close to her mother and father and kept out of trouble.

One afternoon when she was fourteen, Josephine ran to her, "Helen, guess what? Genevieve and I have been invited to the dance the gentlemen farmers are having. It will be such fun.

I know Papa will let me go. I think I'll wear that flowered pink dress. Will you lend me one of your ribbons?"

Just then Mr. Kowalski walked into the room, tired and hungry for his dinner. He smelled one of his favorite suppers.

"Oh, Marianna, what delicious meal are you cooking?"

As he sat down and waited to eat, he joined in Josephine and Helen's conversations.

"Well, Josie, you may go," he said. "But mother tells me poor Genevieve is not feeling well, so Helen must go with you. Isn't that right, Mari?"

"Yes, Stan," she answered, as she placed the overflowing dishes on the table. "Genny has a fever. She can't go out."

Helen and Josie finished eating and went to plan their outfits for the big event. They dressed in their best, they braided each other's hair, and with happy smiles they took off. They had a wonderful time dancing and didn't notice the time. Before they knew it, like Cinderella at the ball, they discovered it was almost midnight. One of the boys walked them home through the dark. They were laughing and talking about the evening when they passed their uncle's house.

Entering their home, they were surprised moments later when their uncle arrived rushing in the door like an angry bull.

"Stan, I must talk to you about your daughters," he exclaimed pounding his fist on the table.

His face was red and his veins were bulging. The girls were huddled together shaking like leaves in a summer storm. To the shock of all the family, he launched into a tirade about

Josephine and Helen being out so late. Mr. Kowalski, embarrassed and ashamed of his daughters, flew into a rage and turned on them in fury. They tried to explain, but he would not listen. He listed their punishment and took out his belt.

"Oh, Papa, I am so sorry," Helen cried sincerely. "I will never do anything to displease you again."

Helen loved her father. She knew he could not understand and felt sad for him that, goaded on by her uncle, he felt he had to punish her and her sister.

She promised herself, "I must not cause him sadness again. I will make up for this somehow. From now on, I will always bring him honor not shame."

This was her resolve and one she never forgot.

"IN SERVICE"

"I am going forward through life amidst rainbows
and storms, but with my head held high with pride,
for I am a royal child. ... I have put my trust
in the mercy of the Lord."

DIARY, 992

The yellow crocus had pushed away the snow, the grass held hints of green, and tiny leaves were bursting forth in the orchard. Soon they would be surrounded by the glory of pink and white blossoms. Helen had hung the clothes on the line and then sat on the backyard bench watching the shirts, pants, and other clothing blow in the soft wind.

She would soon be sixteen years old. As she gazed at a blue dress billowing next to a brown one, she thought, "If I want to attend Mass I have to do something on my own. I can't wear these shabby dresses and Papa doesn't have money for new ones. I'm old enough to go to work like Josephine and Genevieve. That's what I must do — and soon!"

She turned at the creaking of the back door. Her mother walked out carrying a large laundry basket.

"What's on your mind, little girl?" she inquired, as she placed a clothes pin neatly on the corner of a towel.

"Mama," she answered, "Papa works so hard and still I have nothing nice to wear. I am thinking that I would like to go into service so I can earn my own money."

"Helen, I think that could work out. You are almost as old as the other girls were when they left," she answered, as she put her arm around her daughter, "but I hate to think of you leaving us."

Looking toward the village, she added, "You know, Mrs. Gruskalski told me Mrs. Bryszewski is looking for a maid. I could tell her about you, but first let's see what Papa has to say. Now, come help me with these clothes. It's almost time for me to take your father his lunch."

Mrs. Bryszewski lived in a village not too far from the Kowalski's home. She and her husband had a bakery and their little son needed a nanny. Helen's father agreed that she could go.

"Ah, I'll miss her so much, but I know it is time," he told his wife.

After a trip to town and an interview, it was decided Helen would be perfect for the job. She felt grown-up — she was receiving pay — but her life was little changed. It was not much different from what she had done at home. She loved the little boy, cared for him and the house by day, and spent her evenings telling him stories and making him laugh.

Before long, however, Helen had the experience of the strange light in the courtyard and felt God was asking her to do some other work.

Mrs. Bryszewski was puzzled. She did not know about Helen's prayer life. She did not know that she prayed by day and far into the night; she did not know of the strange brightness that kept her awake, and she did not know of the young girl's yearning for God. She only knew that something was wrong, and that her little son would miss his friend. She was afraid that the bizarre and scary incident in the courtyard meant something was seriously wrong.

"Helen, why are you leaving us? We still need you," Mrs. Bryszewski pleaded as she watched Helen pack her things. "Scc, little Joseph is crying."

"I can't tell you why I must leave," she told her employer as she packed, "I am sorry, but I must go home now!"

She wiped the little boy's tears. "Please forgive me. You'll find someone else, Joey, don't worry. God will take care of you."

Her return to the farm was greeted by surprise from her whole family.

"Helen, are you all right?" Genevieve asked, as her sister flew in the door, tossed her bag on the floor, and collapsed on the sofa.

"I'm okay," she replied, "but I must talk to Mama and Papa right away!"

Her parents hurried in from the kitchen where they had been drinking hot milk and wondering about the episode in the courtyard. They looked at their daughter. Her hair was a mess, her eyes were wet. They ran to her.

"Honey, what's the matter?" they asked in unison. "Did the doctor frighten you? Are you sick?"

"No, no, Mama," she answered. "This is good news. I am not sick. I am perfectly well. I just want to enter the convent!"

"What are you saying, Helen?" her father asked. "This is nonsense! It is out of the question! We are poor people. We do not have the money for a dowry," he stormed. "Besides that, we need you here. No, child, you may not even think of it."

"But, Papa, I don't need money. Jesus Himself will lead me to a convent," she countered, as tears spilled from her eyes.

Genevieve held Helen's hands and tried to comfort her. Her little brothers and sisters began to cry and her parents closed their eyes in prayer. They were getting old. Farm folks age early. Marianna was 46 and Stan was 53. Life was taking a toll on them — and Helen was their most helpful and thoughtful child. How could they let her go? God could not ask this sacrifice!

So it was decided. Helen could not disobey her parents. She had to behave like the other girls. Dutifully, she tried. Like a typical teen, she became interested in her appearance and in fashionable clothes. She even joined her girl friends in attending dances — and she attempted to ignore the voice in her soul.

"I must find another position," she thought. "But this time I will find someone who understands me. I must be able to attend Mass every day and I must be allowed to visit the sick and the dying."

She went to Lodz to stay with her uncle. He had been told about her wish to be a sister. He teased her, "Now, now, Helen, are you sure you want to go to the convent? It's no fun there. There aren't any boys, you know." He laughed at her.

"Uncle, I am serious. Boys don't really interest me. I have resolved since I was little to serve God — and that's what I will do," she insisted with a toss of her auburn head.

She found another position and stayed there for a while. Then she went home again and begged her parents to change their minds and let her enter the convent. Once again, they would not hear of it.

Broken-hearted, she returned to Lodz and visited an employment agency, which arranged an interview for a position as a maid. During the interview, Mrs. Sadowski looked at the fashionably dressed girl who did not look like a maid.

She told her, "Well, the pay isn't much, and you would be busy with my three children, especially since I am expecting another child."

Helen looked at the woman and her family. She liked them. They agreed to give her time for Mass and helping others, which she had requested.

"Fine, I'll take it. When can I start?" she asked.

The new maid and baby-sitter was busy most of the time. Mrs. Sadowski owned a grocery store and left the housework to her new girl. The children were lively, but so was Helen and they had great times together. Her storytelling skills amused them, and it seemed she was the perfect help for Mrs. Sadowski in every way.

"You know sometimes I think you should be a comedienne, Lena," Mrs. Sadowski said one day. "You sure know how to make people laugh and be happy."

Helen smiled, "Well, I learned this with my brothers and sisters and the neighbor kids back home. I've been doing it all my life."

Soon after the new baby was born, Helen suddenly told her employer she was leaving.

"Helen, you are like my own daughter. What will I do without you? You have been such a help to me. The children would have been such a handful during my waiting days," Mrs. Sadowski said, as she watched Helen place her clothes in her suitcase. The baby cried fussily in the cradle. As the tired mother picked her up and comforted her, she asked Helen, "How can I let you go?"

Helen reached out and touched her arm. "I wish I could stay longer," she replied, "but I must go. Someday you may understand." She kissed the baby's head and stooped down to hug each little child.

Mrs. Sadowski put her arms around her friend and said, "Helen, we will always remember you."

The children lined up by the gate and waved, Helen lifted her bag in salute and wiped the tears from her eyes.

Helen, too, had had "waiting days" – though not for a baby – and they were soon to end. Midsummer would fade into fall. The green leaves turn orange and red and die away, just as Helen was soon to die to one life and begin another!

THE DANCE

"From today on, I do the Will of God everywhere, always, and in everything."

DIARY, 374

Helen had to talk to someone. She journeyed from Mrs. Sadowski's home to the outskirts of Lodz, where her sister Josephine (now Mrs. Jasinka) lived.

A summer storm blew overhead. It started to rain. Dark clouds and thunder signaled more to come. She hurried through the tree-lined streets and finally reached the young couple's little house. When the door opened to her knock, the drenched girl dropped her damp bag on the porch and fell into her sister's surprised, but welcoming arms.

Immediately, the words rushed out, "Josie, I don't know what to do. I am beset by torment of the soul. I want to — need to — go into the convent. It is what I know I must do. Yet, with

Mama and Papa's feelings, I can't do it. I am so torn!"

"Lena, you have been dealing with this for so long, I know. It must be almost three years since you first asked them," Josephine comforted her.

"Try to stick it out a little longer. Things will work out, you'll see. Now come in, take off those wet clothes. I just made a pot of tea. Sit down with me and we'll talk. Genny and Natalie are coming over soon with some of their friends. It will be great for us girls to get together."

Helen's spirits revived and they were soon laughing happily. The girls came later wearing pretty flowered dresses. They greeted their sister with hugs and kisses and sat down on the sofa.

After catching up on their latest comings and goings, Genny begged her sister, "We're going to a dance now, Lena. It's at the park. Please come with us. We'll all have fun together."

"I think I'd like that," Helen answered. "Give me time to get changed."

She went with them that afternoon, trying her best to hide her spiritual yearnings and to develop a social life as her parents wished.

Helen was a friendly, kind, and thoughtful person who had many friends, and because of her lively personality and beauty she was also attractive to the boys. At social outings, she was very popular — but now she was not as carefree as she appeared to be. She was still troubled inside and prayed as much as ever.

Everybody was having a good time as they danced in the park in the middle of the afternoon, yet her soul was experiencing torments. As she was dancing to the musical beat, smiling at her partner, and tossing her auburn hair, she suddenly saw Jesus at her side — Jesus racked with pain, stripped of His clothing, all covered with wounds. She stopped spinning.

"How long shall I put up with you and how long will you keep putting Me off?" He asked.

At that moment, it was as if the music stopped, the dancers were gone — there remained only Jesus and her. She left the dance in a daze and sat with her sister on the sidelines.

"What's wrong, Lena?" Genevieve asked. "You look pale! Are you okay?"

"Oh, I'm fine. I just have a terrible headache," she answered, placing her hand on her brow and closing her eyes. "I just need to be alone."

She slipped out unnoticed, leaving her sister and all her friends behind and made her way to the nearby Cathedral of Saint Stanislaus Kostka. Only a few people were in the pews; one or two were following the Stations; candles were burning on the altar, but she didn't notice anything that was going on around her. She could think of nothing but Jesus and His words to her.

She fell prostrate before the Blessed Sacrament and begged the Lord, "Dear Jesus, I love You, please help me to understand what's happening. Tell me what I must do now."

Then, she heard these words: "Go at once to Warsaw. You will enter a convent there."

She rose from prayer, left the dark church, and went to Josephine.

She told her sister her experience at the dance. "Oh, Josie, can you understand? Jesus has actually talked to me. Finally, I know what I must do. I can no longer wait for Mama and Papa. I must go to Warsaw. I must go now. Jesus told me to go!"

Helen looked at her sister and begged, "You must break the news to our parents. Tell them I love them."

"Helen, don't worry, I'll do anything for you," Josie replied with a hug. "I'll try to make them understand."

Helen returned to her uncle's home. After exchanging a few words of greeting, she blurted out, "I'm going to Warsaw to enter a convent."

"My God, Helen! What are you doing?" her uncle cried out. "You can't do this! What will your parents say? You know this will make your dear mother and father very sad and break their hearts."

Helen answered, "Please, Uncle, you know how I feel. I have to go! You must tell them after I've gone."

Handing him a large bundle, she added. "When you do get to visit them, please give them this. It is all I own — clothes and things I want my brothers and sisters to have. There is something for each of them."

"And what will you have yourself?" he asked her.

"What I am wearing is enough. Jesus will take care of all my needs."

She wiped her eyes and took hold of his hands. "Uncle, you have been so good to me and I thank you for all you have done. Will you take me to the train station?"

"Of course, if I can't change your mind, I can at least do that," he replied, as he put on his jacket and helped her out to his wagon. Her aunt stood wringing her hands and crying.

The station was not far. They checked the timetable and found they were just in time. A train to Warsaw was bearing down the track just as they arrived.

She was brave until the last minute. Then came more tears.

"Mother will say I ran away from home when she finds out about this," she cried. "I don't want to hurt my parents, but I must be obedient to Jesus. If only they could understand! If only I could make them understand!"

"I will miss them so much," she said to her uncle, as tears spilled down her cheeks. "Tell them I do love them."

"I will. Now, take care of yourself, little one. God be with you," he whispered. The whistle sounded and the train slowly moved down the platform. Her uncle silently watched.

When he arrived home he told his wife, "If the train had waited another minute, I would probably have taken her from it, but it did not. I could only stand there helpless and sad."

It was late evening when the train arrived in Warsaw — so far from home. When she walked out into the station, she was overcome with fear. She had never seen such milling crowds, all going their separate ways — she was terror-stricken!

She looked this way and that. She saw the ticket booths, the long rows of seats — strangers everywhere — and the exit doors leading … where?

"What do I do now?" she thought. "I don't know anyone. Where shall I go?"

She sat on a bench next to a mother and child to gather her thoughts. The little girl smiled at her. Suddenly, she felt safe. She closed her eyes and prayed, "Mary, lead me, guide me."

Immediately, she heard words telling her to leave Warsaw and go to a nearby village where she would find safe lodging for the night. She arose from her seat and went outside where she found transportation to the town. There, everything was just as the Mother of God had told her.

Early the next morning, she arose, returned to the city, and entered the first church she saw, the Church of St. James. She knelt down and began to pray.

"Dear Jesus, show me Your will. I am here in this strange city. You have got to guide me. I don't know where to turn next."

She remained praying for a long time, through several Masses. Then, during one of these Masses, she heard the words, "Go to that priest and tell him everything. He will know what you should do next."

After Mass, she went to the sacristy and asked the priest to advise her. He did, and so began Helen's journey into the unknown.

A WELCOME

"My happiest moments are when I am alone with my Lord."

DIARY, 289

ather Dabrowski followed the altar boys into the sacristy. As he removed his vestments, his mind was on his duties of that day. As a pastor of a large parish he was very busy. He was due at the hospital in an hour to visit one of his parishioners who was dying, then there was that meeting with the bishop downtown, and later the Sodality dinner. He went over the list in his mind as he carefully lifted the robe onto a hanger and put it in the closet.

He was distracted by a gentle tap on the door. An altar boy opened it and peered out. There stood a young girl, somewhat disheveled in appearance.

"Father," said the boy, "someone to see you."

Father Dabrowski walked over. His young visitor looked at him pleadingly. He remembered noticing her praying reverently in a pew near the altar during Mass. He invited her to sit in the armchair over by the stained glass window. After dismissing the altar boys, he pulled up another chair beside her, his head tilted toward her, like a confessor. In fact, he thought she might be in trouble and in need of the sacrament of Penance.

Helen lifted her eyes to his like a puppy with a new master. He realized this was not as he thought. There was something about this girl. There was a glow to her face. He leaned on the arm of his chair, his hand on his chin. He listened intently as her story came out. She told him of her dilemma and that God had singled him out as the one to help her.

"Clearly, this girl has been sent to me," he thought.

Patting her arm, he assured her, "Don't worry. I know God will provide for your future. The main thing now is to get you a place to stay."

He pondered for a few minutes as he studied her, then said, "For the time being, I shall send you to a pious lady who is a friend of mine. Mrs. Lipszyc has four children and is looking for a maid. You will stay with her while you search for the right convent."

Helen smiled, reached for her kerchief, and got up to leave.

"Wait, just a minute, now. I will give you a letter of introduction," he added.

Father reached into a nearby desk and pulled out paper and a pen.

"Aldona," he wrote, "I do not know her, but somehow I feel sure she will qualify. She seems just right for you." This short message was signed, placed in an envelope, and handed to Helen.

He walked over to the window, and pointed out the way to the town of Ostrowek which was not far from Warsaw. "This is where you are to go," he said.

"Oh, thank you, Father," Helen replied with a catch in her voice, "I am so grateful to you." She reached out and kissed his hand.

"I'll be in touch. Just keep your faith in Jesus," he said in good-bye.

Without any difficulty, Helen found her way to Mrs. Lipszyc's home. She arrived with all her possessions tied in a kerchief. Mrs. Lipszyc was in the playroom with her children when she heard the knock. She went to the door where she found a girl only a few years younger than herself. She read the note, which Helen had handed her with a smile, and invited her in.

As they sat on the sofa talking, the sunlight streamed in the window leaving its golden glow on Helen's face. Mrs. Lipszyc found herself moved by this illusion and later would wonder at it. Helen told her story of love for her parents and God's call. She explained that she had left home because she knew Jesus wanted her to enter a convent, and that as soon as she made enough money for her dowry, she would follow His wishes. Mrs. Lipszyc took an immediate liking to the girl who seemed spiritual, cheerful, warm, and kind. She called her children in from their play. They entered the room one by one cautiously, but were soon laughing, captivated by Helen's smile and the funny story she told them.

"My dear, I see you haven't brought much with you," said Mrs. Lipszyc as she noticed Helen's kerchief. "Never mind, we are the same size, and I have plenty of clothes."

She showed Helen her room and listed her duties. The girl was treated like a member of the family from the first moment.

Still, Helen did not intend to stay long. On her time off, she would go into the city and knock like a beggar on the door of one convent after another.

"We do not accept maids here," she was told repeatedly. And because of her lack of education, and her working as a maid, none of the sisters seemed to feel she was qualified — but Helen knew in her heart that Jesus was calling her — and like a faithful handmaiden she would not give up. She searched for "her convent" every free moment and constantly prayed to Jesus, "Help me. Don't leave me alone."

One sunny day, Helen came to the convent of the Sisters of Our Lady of Mercy. The portress answered her knock. She looked out, thrust her head forward like a chicken at a barn door, and asked the pretty young girl, "What do you want, my child?"

Helen looked at her beseechingly and replied, "I wish to enter the convent."

The portress stared at her as she opened the door to allow her guest to enter.

"I can't help you," she stated, "but I will see if Mother Superior is available. Come in and wait here."

She led her visitor to a little dark sitting room. It was sparsely furnished with two chairs and a desk. There was a large crucifix on the wall. Helen prayed with all her heart as she gazed at it.

After a while, Mother Michael entered the room and sat opposite her. Unknown to Helen, the superior had been observing her from the doorway. She felt sure this girl would not be acceptable — although she did seem prayerful.

"Such a fragile little thing," she thought. "I'll listen to her and ask a few questions so as not to hurt her. Then I'll send her on her way."

After a short conversation, Mother became interested in this young girl. She smiled kindly and said, "Child, you must go to the Lord of the house and ask if He will accept you."

It was a strange request, but Helen understood at once that she was to ask this of the Lord Jesus.

"Yes, Mother," she said, as she jumped from her chair and hastened from the room. Somehow she knew where to find the chapel. Candles were burning, but there was no one there praying. She entered and knelt before the golden tabernacle.

"Lord of the house" she prayed, "the sister told me to ask You if You will accept me."

Immediately, she heard a voice, "I do accept you; you are in My Heart."

She quickly got off her knees and rushed to the waiting Mother Superior who was sitting quietly at the desk with her hands folded as in silent prayer. She looked up as the girl walked in.

"Well, has the Lord accepted you?" she questioned.

Helen nodded her head and answered, "Yes."

"If the Lord has accepted you, then I also will accept you," Mother replied to her own surprise, "but there is much that you must do first."

Helen listened as Mother Michael explained what to expect of convent life. She told her that all girls who entered the convent had to have a dowry. She also needed to purchase some changes of clothing. Mother told her how much money she would need. She was staggered by the amount.

"Perhaps you could continue to work and set aside money each week. You could bring it to me from time to time," Mother suggested. "Then, when you have saved enough, you may join us as a postulant."

Helen's eyes watered, "Oh, yes, Mother, thank you. I will do that." She wanted to hug the sister, but instead put out her hand. "Good bye, Mother, you will see, I'll be back soon."

"Oh, yes, my child," she replied. But as she returned to her other duties, Mother Michael soon forgot this strange girl.

Helen ran home to Mrs. Lipszyc with the good news.

"Finally, Aldona, I have found my convent!" she called, as she walked into the kitchen where Mrs. Lipszyc was preparing dinner.

The children gave shrieks of joy. Mrs. Lipszyc wiped her hands on a towel and ran to her.

They sat down at the table and made plans for Helen to start saving her salary.

A few months later, when Mother Michael was away from the convent, she received a letter from one of her sisters. It told her that a young lady had brought in money "for safekeeping, as agreed."

"What is this all about?" she asked her secretary who was standing near her. "Why is someone sending me money? What agreement did I make?"

She slowly reread the words, "... for safekeeping, as agreed." Then she remembered Helen and her visit.

"Well, this is quite a surprise. I completely forgot about that young girl. I never expected to hear from her again. She must be a determined little soul." Then she remarked to no one in particular, "God works in mysterious ways!"

She never forgot Helen again because from then on, the future postulant's deposit kept increasing and within a year she had saved up and sent the sister all the money she needed!

A DREAM COME TRUE

"Mankind will not have peace until it turns with trust to My mercy."

DIARY, 300

*I*t was a sleepy July afternoon. The leaves on the trees barely moved, and a warm breeze intensified the heat. Two glasses of cool lemonade stood on a nearby table, waiting to be sipped. Helen sat on the porch glider reading to the Lipszyc's little girl, swinging slowly back and forth in rhythm with the words. Out of the corner of her eye, she saw the postman walk by and Mrs. Lipszyc go down the path to meet him.

"Good day, Mrs. Lipszyc. Here, I have some letters for you," he said. Aldona reached for her mail and looked through the letters. She smiled.

"Helen, here's one for you. It looks important. Hurry, open it.

Let's read it together."

Helen jumped from the swing, almost spilling the lemonade, and grasped the white linen envelope.

"Oh, Aldona," she screamed, tearing open the envelope. "It's from Mother Michael!" Her eyes scanned the page quickly and she cried, "I'm accepted. Oh, my heart can't stand it! Can you believe it! I'm finally going to enter the convent!"

Aldona felt a tear slip down her cheek. Helen was like a

sister to her, and they had shared so much in the past year. She held Helen tightly, not quite as happy as Helen was.

She remembered that Helen never did get her parents' permission. Only last week they had sent Genevieve to try to dissuade her. Aldona herself felt that marriage to the right young man would be best for her friend. She had even introduced her to some eligible friends of her husband, but Helen was determined to follow Jesus.

"I must be there on August 1, the eve of Our Lady of the Angels," Helen read. "Oh, Aldona, I can't wait! It will be the happiest day of my life!"

Soon the day came that Helen had been awaiting for so many years. The sun smiled that special August morning; the flowers in Aldona's garden nodded good-bye as Helen and Aldona walked to the gate.

"Aldona, I'll always remember all you did for me. I'll pray for you and the children night and day," she stated quietly, stifling a sob. "I love you all. Come and see me. I will miss you so much."

Helen walked into the unknown. She had no idea what convent life was like. She had never really been in a convent before, but she was unafraid. She knew Jesus had directed her there, and she was so happy!

But the life behind the doors was foreign to her. Suddenly, a girl who prayed a lot and visited the church whenever she wished had to ask permission to go to the chapel, and it wasn't often granted; a girl who had been on her own since she was barely fifteen had to learn "holy obedience," and a girl who was outgoing, cheerful, and talkative had to observe "holy silence."

It wasn't long before Helen was confused. She was assigned
to work in the kitchen, where she helped prepare the meals
for the wayward girls in the charge of the Sisters of Our Lady
of Mercy. She had to ready the vegetables; she had to pour
water from the huge pots; she had to scour them, too. She
grew tired and weak. She didn't mind the work exactly, but
she had expected a convent to be prayerful — her days spent
in contemplation of the Lord. It wasn't paradise after all! Now,
she had to learn that work is prayer, too.

After a couple weeks, Aldona came to visit her. She saw a
different girl than she had left only a short time ago. Helen
seemed sad and tired.

"I don't know what to do," the distressed girl said, as she
met her friend in the tiny parlor. Her eyes watered and her hug
was strong and clinging.

"Aldona, I don't think I belong here. Nothing is as I expected
it. I am so mixed-up. Maybe I should just leave."

"Well, Helen, I wish I could help you. You must pray about it
and then do what you feel is right. You can always come back
to me. The children still cry for you, and I miss you, too," she
said as she squeezed her hands in comfort.

Later, Helen thought of what Aldona had said. It wasn't that
she wanted to leave the convent. She wanted to leave *this*
convent! Three weeks had passed and Helen was ready to give
up.

"I will talk to Mother Michael tonight," she told herself. "I will
tell her I must leave and enter a convent of contemplative
sisters. There, I know I'll be happy."

After dinner clean-up in the kitchen, Helen hurried to
Mother's secretary for an appointment, but Mother Michael was
not available that evening. Helen would have to wait until

morning — and she was deeply distressed. She felt she couldn't wait. She ran down the corridor to her "cell" and threw herself on the cold floor in anguish, tears flowing from her eyes.

"Oh, Jesus, help me. I can't take it anymore! I don't know what to do. Please God, I can't stay a minute longer," she gasped. "Tell me what is right. I am so confused! I never thought it would be like this."

Her eyes ached from crying, and her heart ached in misery as she continued to pray. After a while, she noticed a brightness filling her cell. It hurt her eyes even though they were closed. She looked up and saw the very sorrowful Face of Jesus on the curtain. There were open wounds on His Face, and large tears were falling on her white bedspread. Helen stared in wonder.

"Oh, Jesus, who has hurt You so?" she murmured.

She heard His answer, "It is you who will cause Me this pain if you leave this convent. It is to this place that I called you and nowhere else; and I have prepared many graces for you."

Helen sat up, her eyes never left the sorrowing Jesus. A feeling of peace came over her. She actually felt the burden lifting from her shoulders. It was not her decision to make!

"Oh, Jesus, forgive me. You must know I would never hurt You. I will stay here forever if it is Your wish!" she prayed.

The room darkened. Helen fell on her bed exhausted and closed her eyes. For the first time in many days, it was a sound sleep. When the bells awoke her the next morning, she had a new resolve in her heart. She knew she need not speak to Mother Superior.

Later that morning, after she had finished the breakfast dishes, she was given permission by the Mistress of Novices to go to confession.

"What will he say? Will he believe me? Will he think I'm crazy?" she wondered, as she walked into the confessional, knelt down, and blessed herself. With shyness and humility, she told Father all that had taken place.

The old priest listened carefully to the young postulant kneeling before him in the dim church. He knew many girls had a hard time at first. He assured her she was no different from the rest.

"My child," he told her, "I understand. You will be fine. I am sure it is God's will that you stay with the Sisters of Our Lady of Mercy. From what you have told me, there must be work for you here. You must not even think about leaving." With that, he gave her absolution.

"Go, my daughter, and serve the Lord," he said, as he closed the sliding panel.

On hearing this, Helen closed her eyes and breathed a loud sigh of relief. She left the confessional and walked calmly up to the altar to say her penance. She knelt before the statue of the Sacred Heart.

"Jesus, thank You. I know now that I can handle whatever is to come because You are ever beside me showing me the way. I will be more patient and try my best without always questioning. I will follow Your example. Your life was not always easy. I know how You suffered, and I will bear with my suffering, too," she prayed.

Helen returned to the kitchen. A song filled her heart. She felt happy and at peace.

SISTER FAUSTINA

"Let God push your boat out into the deep waters, toward the unfathomable depths of the interior life."

DIARY, 55

Spring was in full bloom in Cracow, and Helen's heart was as light and airy as the apple blossoms swaying in the wind outside her window. As she gazed at the soft veil and the snowy white gown which she was wearing, she thought of the day of her First Holy Communion — the dress her mother had made, the candles glowing, the golden tabernacle. She remembered how she had walked home from the little church in the village that day so long ago, thinking only of Him. Though as a little girl she had loved Jesus, little did she dream that someday in the future she would be His bride. Today she was wearing her wedding gown and her spouse was Jesus. She loved Him so much, and she knew He loved her.

The past eight months had been hard in spite of her resolve to stick it out. Many times she had wondered if she was doing the right thing. Often Jesus seemed so far away. Though she tried her best, she couldn't quite reach Him. She was sure He was there, but beyond her touch — like a hand across the water inches away from a drowning person.

"Come closer, come closer," her heart begged.

Oh, but this day was different!

"Isn't it wonderful!" she said to her friend Daria as they dressed. "I am so excited! Even though my parents got my letter too late to come like yours, nothing can calm me down. Just think – in a couple minutes, we will walk up that aisle like brides — and then we will get our habits! I won't be 'Helen Kowalska' any more — you can call me 'Sister [Maria] Faustina of the Most Blessed Sacrament.' I love the sound of that name."

Solemnly, the white-gowned girls walked up the aisle of the glowing church — the many brides of the Lord. Their eyes shone, their gowns rippled. The pews were filled with family and friends, wiping tears from their eyes.

Helen stood joyfully before the altar waiting to accept the religious habit and receive her new name. Suddenly, she fainted. The other postulants knelt while she slipped helplessly onto the floor. For a moment, confusion reigned.

"Helen, are you okay?" the sister standing nearby asked, as the others quickly surrounded her and helped her to rise.

"Oh yes, I'm fine. I'm so sorry," she answered shakily, as she stood up, trying to regain her bearing — and the ceremony went on normally.

All went well after that. They gathered in the parlor when it was over, but again Helen became faint as she was being dressed in the habit of a novice of the Sisters of Our Lady of Mercy. All the girls were laughing happily, busy changing their clothes when it happened.

"Helen, what's the matter?" asked her friend. "Are you sorry to leave the world?"

She shook her head. She couldn't tell them. They could never understand. They might not even believe her. While her eyes were closed, she had had a vision. She clearly saw how much she was going to suffer in future days. For a moment, tears filled her eyes. She was scared.

She had thought she would always be happy once she had reached her dream. What now? How could she bear what she had seen?

Then it was gone, almost as though it never happened. She experienced that moment of knowledge, then God filled her soul with great joy. She finished dressing along with the other postulants. She put it out of her mind. How could she be unhappy? She had made it this far, she shouldn't worry about what was to come — she was now a novice!

As the days passed, the same girl who had charmed the children she had cared for, had a positive effect on all around her, because of her joy and her enthusiasm. Her companions liked and admired her, and at recreation gladly grouped themselves around her. She fascinated them. She could tell a story interestingly and always knew how to speak about God and spiritual matters.

The new Sister Faustina spent her time in prayers and learning, at the same time she continued working in the kitchen. Though she seemed happy on the outside, this year had hard moments, too. Often, she had to make a great effort to meditate and pray. At times she was greatly troubled.

"Jesus, my Spouse, do You not see that my soul is dying because of its longing for You? How can You hide Yourself from a heart that loves You so sincerely?" she prayed.

But God was silent.

Two years went by quickly. Not long after Easter, on the 30th of April, 1928, Faustina made her first vows. Offering herself to God was an immense effort even though she loved Him with all her heart.

The young novices again walked to the altar, this time to make promises for one year. Once again the church was filled. As Faustina was being clothed with the black veil, her doubts disappeared, and joy overcame her. Finally, she felt His presence close to her. It was visible on her face!

This time her parents were able to be with her. As they had made their way to the convent, they had planned how they would convince her to change her mind.

"Marianna," spoke Stanislaus, "This is wrong for Helen. We both know it. We must talk her out of this nonsense. I want her to come home with us today. Just think how happy this will make the whole family."

Marianna looked at him and nodded her head, "Perhaps you are right, Stan, but you know Helen, she has a mind of her own. She hasn't listened to us for a long time."

They arrived at the convent and went into church. There, they saw the future nuns lined up going up the aisle. They had not seen their daughter for years. They searched the candle-lit church until they saw her near the front pew.

Marianna leaned over to her husband. She touched his hand.

"Oh Stan, there she is. Look over there to the right. Do you see her, Stan?" whispered Marianna. "She looks like an angel. How beautiful she is! Her face is glowing." She shook her head as she gazed at the girl, "Is this really our little Helen?"

"I see her. Oh, Mari, what can I say?" Stan replied, as he watched the ceremony, "I have a feeling she will never leave here. We taught her to love Jesus. Now, she is in love with Him — just like our other girls love their husbands. She belongs to Him. Mari, I have never seen anything like this."

He put his arm around his wife and wiped a tear from his eyes. "This is the will of God," pronounced her father.

Faustina burst through the crowd of happy parents and friends awaiting the girls after the ceremony. She threw herself into their arms.

"Oh Mama, Papa, oh, I am so happy to see you." Her tears mingled with theirs and they hugged each other time and again.

"Helen, we are so proud of you. You did what you had to do. Now I see you were right," said her Papa. "You have our blessing."

She put her arms around them and cried in joy.

"Papa, thank you, thank you," she murmured, as her head lay on his shoulder. "You have made this the happiest day of my life. You finally understand!"

She took her mother's hand and all three strolled through the garden. She asked about the rest of the family, but it seemed no other words were necessary. They were at peace together.

As she kissed them good-bye, she said with a smile, "You see, Papa, you will have sons-in-law and grandchildren through your other daughters. Genny, Josie, Natalie, Mary, and Wanda will soon fill your house with children, but don't forget the One whose bride I am is my husband and your son-in-law, too." Her father wept.

"Mari," he told his wife as they headed home, "I am sorry now that we didn't help Helen to realize her dream. We made it so difficult for her." He bowed his head in sorrow.

He looked lovingly at his wife and then heavenward.

"Now I'm thankful she knows it was only our love for her. God had asked us for this sacrifice, and we fought Him. At last, we are finally giving our daughter to Him."

"I know, Stan," she answered, "I'm sure Helen understands. She is so full of love. I am so proud of our little girl. She is the chosen one. Do you remember what I told you the day she was born! As soon as I saw that little bundle, I knew."

After they left, the orphan girls whom the Sisters of Our Lady of Mercy cared for had a celebration for the new sisters.

"Look at Sister Faustina," one young orphan said, as she served the cookies. "Her face is shining. Will we ever be so happy?"

"Maybe someday we will be when we get out of this place and are on our own. She is my model. She is always kind and thoughtful. Even when she is tired from her hard work in the kitchen, she still has time for us," her friend said.

That night, when Faustina returned to her cell, she thought about the advice her confessor had given her that morning. She would make it her motto.

"Go through life doing good," he had told her. "Act in such a way that all those who come in contact with you will go away joyful. Sow happiness about you because you have received much from God. Give, then, generously to others."

There were times in future days when she would be hard put to keep these words in mind. Her spirituality was frowned on and misunderstood by some of her superiors and some of the other girls. Why did she always want to go to the chapel? they wondered. But Faustina had always been different. She realized that. She was burning with love for Jesus. She prayed with all her heart. She spoke to Jesus day and night. Though there were times His mother Mary came and comforted her, she longed for Jesus. And soon she would be rewarded.

THE DIVINE MERCY

"I will tell you most when you converse with Me in the depths of your heart."

DIARY, 581

It was February 22, 1931, a cold night in Poland. Sister Faustina had been in the convent for four and a half years. She pondered this as she returned to her room after evening prayers in the chapel. The wind howled like a lonely wolf outside her window and snowflakes danced in the dark night. She shivered and pulled her shawl tightly around her shoulders as she entered her chilly cell — a room sparsely furnished with only a cot and a chest. Her bed looked warm and inviting as she prepared for sleep and knelt to say her prayers.

Then came a moment that changed her life. It was the moment she learned her mission and why God had sent her there. As she lifted her eyes in prayer to the crucifix, Jesus appeared before her. Her folded hands opened, and she gripped the bed. She gasped at the sight of Jesus. He was dressed in a white robe. As He looked at her, His right hand was raised in a gesture of blessing, the other was pointing to His heart. From his heart there were shining two large rays, one red, the other pale.

In silence she waited, staring at her Lord while her heart was filled with great joy. After a while, Jesus spoke.

He said, "Paint an image according to the pattern you see, with the signature, 'Jesus, I trust in You.' I desire this image be venerated, first in your chapel and then throughout the entire world."

Barely moving and almost holding her breath, she listened carefully to His instructions. She understood that God had a plan for her, and finally she knew it.

Turning to her with love in His eyes, He added, "I promise that the soul that will venerate this image will not perish. I also promise victory over its enemies already here on earth, especially at the hour of death. I Myself will defend it as My own glory."

With that He was gone.

Sister Faustina had been frozen to her bed. When Jesus left, His words were engraved on her heart — but she must not forget them or any detail of the beautiful Jesus. She was exhilarated, but also puzzled. She was not an artist. She had never touched paints in her entire life! Though she tried to sleep, all night she lay awake tossing and turning wondering how she could accomplish what had been asked of her.

The next morning she arose at the bell, joined the others at morning prayers, and worked in the kitchen. At the first chance, she ran to talk to a priest. She needed to talk to someone, for thoughts had been running around in her brain like humming bees all morning, and she couldn't say a word to the other girls. As one word ran into the other, she told the priest what had happened.

He listened to her tale, then spoke kindly, "Now, Sister, calm down. You must realize Jesus refers to your soul. You must paint God's image in your soul. He doesn't actually want you to take a brush in hand. Try to do what is right for your soul and He will be happy with you. Now, go in peace."

When she came out of the confessional, she walked like a sleepwalker thinking of Father's words. She knelt before the altar and with a soft voice thanked God that she now understood His wishes.

Then, she heard the words, "My image already is in your soul. I desire that there be a Feast of Mercy. I want this image, which you will paint with a brush, to be solemnly blessed on the first Sunday after Easter; that Sunday is to be the Feast of Mercy.

"I desire that priests proclaim this great mercy of Mine towards the souls of sinners. Let the sinner not be afraid to approach Me. The flames of Mercy are burning Me — clamoring to be spent. I want to pour them out upon these souls."

Sister Faustina lifted her eyes to the golden tabernacle. Jesus was giving her a mission — she knew it. She had not misunderstood Him. She had to do something, but what? She couldn't go back into the confessional, but she had to talk to someone!

It was afternoon. Sunlight streamed through the stained glass window. She still had time before she had to prepare supper. She knew Mother Superior would be in her office. Leaving the chapel, the girl walked quickly down the hall, and knocked timidly on the oak door. Mother opened it and looked at a puzzled Sister who seemed to be crying.

"Come in, Sister. What is wrong?" she asked, as she put on her glasses and peered at her visitor.

Sister Faustina told her all the details of what had happened both with Jesus and then Father in the confessional.

"Mother Rose," she begged, "What should I do?"

Mother shook her head. This girl was very spiritual and close to God, but was she hallucinating? Was Jesus really appearing to her?

"You must ask the Lord Jesus for a sign proving that this request really comes from Him."

Evidently Jesus gave Mother a sign, for the next day she supplied her little novice with artist materials — many tubes and brushes. Faustina had never painted, she didn't know where to start, but she tried her best to duplicate what she had seen. Though she worked very hard in all her free moments, covering the canvases with color and design, she finally realized it was hopeless. Nothing she did was right — her room and her hands were a mess — and her attempts were like a mockery of the beautiful Jesus who had visited her.

Mother Superior came to her cell to see how she was doing.

"Oh, Mother, look at this," she said, as she showed her the unsightly canvasses, "What can I do? Do you think Jesus does not want me personally to paint the picture? Can someone else do it?"

Mother nodded her head in agreement. This young woman was not an artist!

Meanwhile, when word spread around the convent, the sisters whispered about it and they began to look at her as hysterical. They felt she was a fanatic, and they did not believe in her vision. Faustina knew how they felt and wished she could explain. Once again, she knew she was not crazy, but she had to bear everything in silence, being patient with those who were accusing her. Jesus had His reasons even if she could not understand them completely.

"Jesus," she prayed, "I am trying as best I can to do everything with the purest of intentions." But life was hard for her.

Satan took advantage of her, and discouragement entered her mind.

"Jesus, Jesus, I cannot go on any longer," she cried one night when she got to her cell and fell on her face before the crucifix. She broke out in a sweat and was overcome by fear. She had no one to turn to. Suddenly, she heard a voice within her soul, "Do not fear; I am with you."

She understood that she should not give in to the temptation to give up. She knew that Jesus would give her the strength and courage to do His wishes.

Many times after that Jesus appeared and consoled her. He taught her a prayer which He called the Chaplet of Divine Mercy. He assured her of His love and comforted her in her suffering.

But the painting had to wait. Life as a sister had to go on for Faustina. She still had her duties to perform and her studying to do. It was all in Mother Superior's hands now.

On May 1, 1933, Faustina would take her perpetual vows. Then she would truly be a Sister of Our Lady of Mercy. Just before taking the vows, the sisters would lay prostrate before the altar and would be covered with a large piece of black cloth, with a white cross in the middle. It was a symbol of being "dead to the world and its enticements." At the same time, the bells would toll as in a funeral and the community would recite Psalm 129, which is also recited at funerals. The bishop would then sprinkle the prostrate sisters with holy water and say, "Rise, you are dead to the world, and Jesus Christ will give you light."

The church pews were filled with people — sisters, students, invited guests, and relatives of the sisters sharing the moment with someone they loved. Sister Faustina had no one there. Her family could not afford the money for the trip, but she did not mind. Once again she was alone with Jesus — just as on her Holy Communion Day — and that was enough.

After the profession, Mother Superior felt it was time to again work on the painting. She sent for Father Sopocko who listened to the directions Jesus had given Sister Faustina in 1931. He wanted to check her mental condition and felt she should be examined by a doctor. After the examination, Sister Faustina was declared to be of sound mind, so Father Sopocko was willing to proceed.

"I believe this is truly from God," he confided to Mother Superior. "I know a neighborhood artist who could work with you."

Three years had passed since Jesus had appeared in the Vision of Divine Mercy, but finally on January 2, 1934, Father Sopocko commissioned Eugene Kazimirowski to paint the image. Mother Superior allowed Sister Faustina to work with the artist. Each week, with Mother Superior or another sister, she would visit his study and describe what she had seen. Father Sopocko was the only other person to hear Sister Faustina's instructions.

Jesus had also commanded Sister Faustina to celebrate the Feast of Mercy on the first Sunday after Easter. That year it was on Sunday, April 8, 1934. The artist worked for months hoping to have it completed on time, but the painting was not done until June.

Finally, came the unveiling. When Faustina saw that the finished painting was not as beautiful as the Jesus of her vision, she was very sad. Weeping, she went to the chapel. She knelt in a pew near the door and put her face in her hands.

"Oh, Jesus," she sobbed, "who will paint You as beautiful as You are?"

Then, she heard the words, "Not in the beauty of the color nor the brush lies the greatness of this image, but in My grace."

She raised her wet eyes to the altar in thanksgiving and in relief left the chapel knowing Jesus was pleased with her.

When the painting was completed, it was placed in the corridor of the convent of the Bernardine Sisters near the church of St. Michael, where Father Sopocko was rector. There it remained for a long time. Through the next several years, Saint Maria Faustina continued to live every moment of her life totally for Jesus. Even though her sickness kept her in and out of hospitals, she never complained. She always tried to do her part even when she was in great pain. Some of the sisters did not understand her and thought she was pretending to be very sick. They made cruel remarks and accused her falsely. These hurt her as much as the coughing and pain in her side. Through it all, she relied on Jesus who reminded her that He too was unjustly accused.

It wasn't until April 3, 1937 that the painting was finally blessed and hung in church, the prayers Jesus had taught her were said in public, and Jesus' desire that the Feast of Divine Mercy be observed throughout the entire world had its beginning.

CHAPTER 11

FINALLY, WITH JESUS

"My daughter, My favor rests in your heart."

DIARY, 1774

October 5, 1938, dawned, the blue morning sky smiled and sunshine poured its warm rays on a sleeping young woman. She opened her eyes and glanced about her, happy to see she was no longer at the sanitarium, but home with her sisters at the convent. Too weak to rise from her cot, she gazed at the crucifix hanging over her bed and silently said her morning prayers.

Sister Faustina's thirteen years in the convent had passed quickly. She had been suffering with tuberculosis for several years and now lay on her death bed. She no longer was able to eat. She knew soon she would be with Jesus in heaven.

During the day, many sisters dropped by to see to her. At four o'clock, Father Andrasz heard her confession. Though surrounded by love, pain still enfolded her like a dark cloud.

The nurse saw her discomfort and came close to her bed. "Sister, how about if I give you a needle?" she asked. "It will help you to sleep."

Sister Faustina agreed, but a few minutes later when the nurse returned, she had changed her mind.

"No, Sister," she stated emphatically as she turned away from the injection and closed her eyes, "I must suffer like Jesus did." The needle was returned to the cabinet.

Like many saints before her who endured suffering patiently, she thought, "I will concentrate on Jesus and His goodness. I will recall the many moments in my life where He has guided and supported me."

Like a bright kaleidoscope, bits and pieces of her life danced through her mind — her holy parents, her loving brothers and sisters, her First Communion, so many moments with Jesus.

Her mind raced back to her childhood. Even as a very little girl, she had been conscious of the "light" that came in the night. Though her parents had told her to stop imagining things, she knew it was real.

She remembered the time she had longed to go to Mass and had frightened the whole family when she made an early trip to the barnyard.

She thought of Jesus appearing to her at the dance and how He had guided her to Warsaw and enabled her to finally reach her dream.

She wondered at her fears and disappointments during those first days in the convent. Even then, she was not strong.

She smiled as she thought of the time she had been so weak she could hardly lift the pot of potatoes when working in the kitchen. When she went to the chapel and complained like a troublesome child to Jesus, He told her He would help her. The next time she attempted to pour the water off, the huge pot seemed light. When she lifted the lid, inside were the most beautiful roses she had ever seen. She could still see them and smell their fragrance — and the pots were never too heavy again!

She remembered the many times He had appeared to her and how they had shared long conversations in her cell at night when all were asleep. Oh, she loved Him so much! She had lived every day of her life for her Jesus. Even in times of distress, things always worked out when she trusted Him.

Her thoughts turned to her family. They were not to be told she was dying. The trip would be long and expensive, and it didn't matter now. She recalled the wonderful visit she had had with them four years ago.

It had started out sadly. A letter had arrived saying her mother was dying. Mother Superior quickly made arrangements so she could be with her family. The trip seemed to take forever. When she arrived at the little cottage, she barely said hello to the others as she hopped from the car, opened the door, and ran to her mother's room.

Her father sat beside the bed while a woman she barely recognized lay bundled in a blue blanket. Placing her arms around the frail woman, she cried, "Oh Mother, your Helen is here." Her mother looked up in surprise at the sight of her daughter, and brightened when she heard the words, "Mama, I love you so much!"

"Helen, is it really you? Are you really here?" She turned to her husband. "Stan, am I dreaming?" she asked.

With tears filling her eyes, Faustina hugged her. "Yes, Mama, it is me. It really is your little Helen!"

With that Mrs. Kowalski sat up in bed. She put her arms around her daughter and cried. All sickness seemed to leave her. She reached for her husband and took his hand.

"Stan, I'm hungry," she announced happily. Within moments, all the family entered the room to see their mother was well once more. The next day they went to church together. She never did have the operation her doctor had said she needed.

Looking back now on all those happy moments made the pain go away. During her visit everybody wanted to be with her. Her parents were always by her side. Her brothers sang and strummed their musical instruments. Her sisters and nieces and nephews played games — and they all went to Mass together. It was like the old days!

But all the happy memories in the world could not cure Faustina. She knew her mission in this life was now over. The painting had been venerated and many of the sisters were praying the Divine Mercy Chaplet daily. She had followed His wishes in everything. Now she was getting very tired. Her eyes didn't want to stay open.

Nine o'clock came. The pain had calmed. Her cough had subsided. Darkness had descended and blessed candles were lit on the small table next to her bed. The shadows on the wall flickered like angels standing watch over her. The sisters and the chaplain knelt and said the prayers for the dying. Then, with tear-filled eyes, each said her good-bye. Faustina, who just that morning had told Sister Felicia, "The Lord will take me today," held each one close and murmured a few words of comfort.

"Let her rest now," cautioned Mother Superior, as she led the sisters from the room.

Only Sister Liguoria remained. She sat on a hard chair near the bed. Like a loving mother caring for her child, she fingered her rosary beads and tenderly kept watch over her friend. It had been a long day and she was tired. She had seen Sister Faustina suffer so much lately and her heart ached for her. As Liguoria prayed the words of the Chaplet of Divine Mercy, "Eternal Father, I offer You the Body and Blood, Soul and Divinity of Your dearly beloved Son ...", she stared at the blinking candles and her eyes began to close.

Suddenly something aroused her. She reached for Faustina's hand and quickly knelt by the bed. She glanced at the clock. It was 10:43. Mother had gone to bed and Liguoria knew she must get her right away! She raced from the room. As she left, another sister was awakened and went into the infirmary to see Faustina. Faustina opened her eyes. She seemed to hear a sound. Her eyes searched the room. She smiled, breathed deeply, closed her eyes, and died. A bright glow appeared on her face. Suddenly, all signs of pain or suffering were gone. Faustina was young and beautiful!

Sister Liguoria came back to the room, with Mother Superior.

"Oh, Mother," said the sister as tears streamed down her cheeks. "Look at her face! See how it shines!"

"Yes," replied Mother Superior as she embraced Liguoria. "She is gone from us, but she is with her Jesus at last and His light radiates from her."

The others returned, walking in solemn procession into the room. They prayed by her bed, but Faustina was no longer there. Her suffering was over and she was on her way to heaven!

Saint Maria Faustina's funeral took place two days later on October 7, 1938, the Feast of the Holy Rosary. After Mass, her fellow sisters and the girls carried her coffin on their shoulders and sadly laid Sister Faustina to rest in the convent cemetery beyond the garden.

CHRONOLOGY

1905   August 25, born in Glogowiec, Poland.
          August 27, baptized in St. Casimir Church.

1912   At age seven hears first call from God.

1914   Receives First Holy Communion.

1917   November, begins education.

1921   At age sixteen, begins "in service."

1922   Announces to parents desire to enter a convent;
          parents refuse permission.

1922-24 Continues to work "in service."

1924   Goes to Warsaw, applies at Sisters of Our Lady
          of Mercy.

1925   August 1, accepted by Sisters of Our Lady of Mercy.

1928   April 30, makes first temporary vows.

1931   February 22, sees vision of the Lord Jesus as
The Divine Mercy. He tells her to paint an image
according to the vision.

1933   May 1, makes perpetual vows.

1934   January 2, visits artist Kazimirowski who is to paint
The Divine Mercy image.
June, painting completed.
October 26, sees vision of The Divine Mercy again
in the garden.

1935   February 15, visits seriously ill mother.

1936-38 Suffers serious health problems.

1938   October 5 at 10:45 PM, goes to her reward in Heaven.
October 7, funeral.

1992   March 7, declared "venerable" by the Church.

1993   April 18, beatified by Pope John Paul II. It is on the
first Sunday after Easter, the Feast of Divine Mercy.

2000   April 30, canonized by Pope John Paul II.
Once again, it is the first Sunday after Easter, the
Feast of Divine Mercy.

GLOSSARY

absolution — a remission of sin.

alms — money, food, or other donations given to the poor and needy.

auburn — reddish brown or golden brown color.

audible — capable of being heard.

austere — severe in appearance.

authorities — persons having the legal power to make and enforce the law.

beseechingly — imploring urgently.

beset — to attack on all sides.

billowing — puffing up.

bon voyage — to wish someone a pleasant trip.

bulging — swelling or bending outward.

catechism — an elementary book containing questions and answers on the principles of a Christian religion.

cautiously — using caution or care.

cell — a small room in a convent.

charges — someone committed to one's care.

clamoring — uttering noisily.

coffin — the box in which the body of a dead person is buried.

collapsed —fell down from exhaustion.

comedienne — a woman who is a comic entertainer or an actress.

commune — to converse or talk together.

conflict — controversy or quarrel.

contemplated — considered thoughtfully.

contemplative — a person devoted to contemplation.

convent — a community of people, especially nuns, devoted to religious life under a superior.

countered — refuted another person's statement.

courtyard — a court open to the sky usually enclosed on all four sides.

crucifix — a cross with the figure of Jesus on it.

destitute — lacking food, clothing, and shelter.

devised — to contrive or to plan.

dilemma — a situation requiring a choice.

disheveled — unkempt, untidy, disarranged.

dowry — money or goods required for marriage or entering a convent.

dramatize — to express oneself in an exaggerated way.

dynasty — the rule of a family or group.

ebbing — flowing backward or away.

eligible — a proper or a worthy choice; desirable.

emanating — flowing out.

embellished — enhanced.

enticements — something that tempts.

exhilarated — gladdened; enlivened.

fanatic — a person with extreme zeal.

fragrance — a pleasing scent.

goaded — urged.

glider — a porch swing suspended from above.

hallucinating — experiencing a false notion, belief, or impression.

hysterical — uncontrollable emotions.

insanity — unsoundness of mind.

intently — with strong attention.

kerchief — a woman's square scarf used as a covering for the head or shoulders.

level-headed — having common sense and sound judgment.
loft — a room within a sloping roof; an attic.
lugging — pulling or carrying with effort.

monstrance — a receptacle used in the Roman Catholic
    Church to display the Sacred Host.
muggy — oppressively humid; damp and close.
mused — thought or meditated in silence.

nanny — a child's nursemaid.

ominously — threatening to harm.

parish — a local church.
parishioner — member of a parish.
pastor — a priest in charge of a church.
perches — a place for a person or animal to rest upon.
perish — to die as a result of violence; to pass away or
    disappear.
pious — showing a reverence for God.
portress — a woman who has charge of the door.
postulant — a candidate for admission to a religious order.
prostrate — to cast oneself face down on the ground.
psalms — sacred songs or hymns.

raffle — a lottery in which a number of persons buy one or
    more chances to win a prize.
ravaged — damaged severely.
recitation — a reciting or repeating something from memory.

sacristy — a room in a church where sacred vessels and
    vestments are kept.
sanitarium — a hospital for the treatment of tuberculosis.
saturated —soaked completely.

self-determination — freedom of a people to determine the way in which they will be governed.

sparsely — scantily, meagerly.

stanzas — the arrangement of lines in a poem.

stymied — hindered or blocked.

tabernacle — an ornamental receptacle for the Eucharist.

thrashed — beat in punishment.

tirade — a prolonged outburst.

torment — agony.

tranquil — calm.

trepidation — tremulous fear.

tuberculosis — a disease affecting the lungs.

unison — at the same time; all at once.

vehemently — with great energy and anger.

venerate — to treat with reverence.

Vespers — a religious service in the late afternoon or evening.

vivid — strikingly bright or brilliant.

wafted — carried lightly and smoothly through the air.

wayward — rejecting what is right and proper; disobedient.

wracked — damaged or destroyed.

wreath — a circular band of flowers.

yearnings — having a strong or earnest desire.

INDEX

ABOUT THE AUTHOR

CLAIRE JORDAN MOHAN, formerly of King of Prussia and Lansdale, now resides in Chalfont, Pennsylvania with her husband, Robert. Having retired from full-time teaching at Visitation B.V.M. School in Trooper, PA, she spends her time writing, traveling, and enjoying her grandchildren. She is a CCD teacher at her parish and a tutor at Graterford Prison. She has had many articles published in magazines and newspapers and has appeared on national radio and television shows, including Mother Angelica Live, the 700 Club and CNBC. On a recent trip to Rome for the Beatification of Blessed Frances Siedliska, Claire Mohan presented a special edition of her book *A Red Rose for Frania* to Pope John Paul II. Her recent book *The Young Life of Pope John Paul II* was also hand-delivered to Our Holy Father.

She is the mother of five children and grandmother of twelve. Claire is a graduate of Little Flower High School and is a 1984 *summa cum laude* graduate of Villanova University where she was valedictorian of her class. She attended West Chester University and Chestnut Hill College for graduate studies. Claire Jordan Mohan welcomes interviews and speaking engagements.

ABOUT THE ILLUSTRATOR

JANE ROBBINS' clean, sharp illustrations reflect her classical training. An art major in high school, she was awarded a scholarship to Moore College of Art. She studied at Philadelphia College of Art, and Fleisher's Memorial in Philadelphia, Baum School in Allentown, and Bishop University in Quebec. She taught painting at the YWCA in Philadelphia and has held private art classes in her home.

In addition to Claire Mohan's current book, Mrs. Robbins illustrated Mrs. Mohan's previous books, *The Young Life of Pope John Paul II*, *The Young Life of Mother Teresa of Calcutta*, and *Give Me Jesus* as well as *Redheads*. Also, she has written and illustrated articles for magazines. The winner of numerous awards, her work is in private collections throughout the United States and Canada.

OTHER BOOKS
by Claire Jordan Mohan

The Young Life of Pope John Paul II
Young and old will enjoy this story which details the young life of Pope John Paul II while a boy in Poland. The way Karol Wojtyla handles the triumphs of his life will inspire children to emulate this courageous boy. They learn his life was just like theirs — a mixture of sadness and joy. They meet "a real boy" who shares their hobbies and interests and in the end, grows up to be a most respected religious and world leader.

The Young Life of Mother Teresa of Calcutta
How Gonxha Agnes Bojaxhiu grew to be a world famous personage and a living example of Jesus in a dark world is the basis for this new book for young and old to treasure. This story gives insight into the people and events in Mother Teresa's young life that shaped the final woman — the early death of her beloved father, Nikola, a political figure in the days of unrest of Yugoslavia — her mother, the warm hospitable Dronda, who always had time for others. We learn how a "pretty mischievous young tomboy" eventually became a world revered "living saint."

A Red Rose for Frania
This children's book offers young readers a thoughtful, endearing story of Frances Siedliska's joys and struggles on her pathway to sainthood. This story demonstrates courage and perseverance as it describes Frania's poor health and obstacles in committing to religious life.

Kaze's True Home
This delightful story of the young life of Maria Kaupas will inspire each child as young Casimira follows her star to attain "the impossible dream." "Kaze" as she was called, was neither wealthy nor did she enjoy the opportunities of the young people of today, but she loved God and was able to share her love with others.

Give Me Jesus
A book that can be appreciated by any age, child or adult. Beautiful selections from authors past and present. It is a magical assortment of special prayers, reflections, and stories that focus on God's love for us. An inspiring tool in giving children building blocks to faith, as well as a trip down memory lane for their parents.

St. Maximilian Kolbe: The Story of the Two Crowns
St. Maximilian Kolbe is known throughout the world today for giving his life for another amid the horrors of the concentration camp in World War II. Raymond Kolbe's life as a young boy, the questions raised by the appearance of Mary, and all the events of his life leading to this crucial moment are brilliantly recounted by the author in this inspiring story told through the eyes of the man saved from the "starvation bunker" in Auschwitz.

WHAT OTHERS ARE SAYING ...

About ... The Young Life of Pope John Paul II
"... a delightful read for children ... leads the reader into the very soul of that deeply introspective and brilliant young man."
— Catholic Library Association

"... this is a splendid little book. Children will enjoy it at home and from the school library."   — The Upper Peninsula Catholic

About ... The Young Life of Mother Teresa of Calcutta
"... not only a pleasant introduction to Mother Teresa ... but also an inspiring introduction to the life and works of all missionaries ... The love and compassion shown in Mother Teresa's quotations will strengthen everyone who reads them." —Catholic Library Association

"Here is a lovely book written for children about Mother Teresa ... packed with beautiful images to provoke our imagination."
— T.O.R.C.H. Book Reviews

About ... Kaze's True Home
"We live in an era rampant with violence, hate, and fear where the media gives the impression that everyone is corrupt and evil. It is very refreshing to read a story about a contemporary who is a real live saint. A ray of sunshine in a dark world!   A marvelous job!"
  — Peter A. Mankas, Director, Lansdale Public Library, Lansdale, PA

"I enjoyed reading the book. I found it interesting, and exciting to follow Casimira on her journeys' — though it also made me cry."
— Rachel Galie, Visitation BVM School, Trooper, PA

About ... Give Me Jesus

"I really like this book."
— Heather Hinkle, Twin Oaks Elementary School

"This collection is broad and embracing, touching a variety of inner worlds. It is colorful, playful, intimate, and expressive ... As an editor, I find this work delightful."
— Kass Dotterweich, Liguori Publications

"This book of prayers for children is very inspiring. It presents poems for enjoyment and memorization — a delight!"
> — Theresa Johnson, Catholic Heritage Curricula

About ... St. Maximilian Kolbe: The Story of the Two Crowns

"... I found this story inspirational. In a world filled with intolerance, St. Maximilian Kolbe was a wonderful example of acceptance, bravery, and love. Hopefully, all those who read the story will model their lives after him."
> — Loretta J. Halas, teacher Grade 7, Cedarbrook Middle School, Elkins Park, PA.

"This book is one of my favorites and I advise everyone who loves to read to take a look at it. The facts poured out, with fun twists to them. I learned so much about a great man and enjoyed every page of this book.
> — Drew Wilkens, Grade 5, Pine Run Elementary School, Doylestown, PA.

"I loved this story! — Learned some things as well."
> — Margaret F. McMenamin, Director of Religious Education, St. Jude School, Chalfont, PA.